I0134232

FINISHING LINE PRESS

www.finishinglinepress.com

# The Body, Like Bread

*poems by*

## Cati Porter

*Finishing Line Press*
Georgetown, Kentucky

# The Body, Like Bread

ACKNOWLEDGMENTS

*No Tell Motel:* "Only the Pots Know the Boiling Point of Their Broth"
*Contrary Magazine:* "Falling In, Falling Out"; "Grace"
*The Quotable Lit:* "Reciprocity"




Editor: Christen Kincaid

Cover Art: Lavina Blossom

Author Photo: Scott Russell

Cover Design: Elizabeth Maines


Printed in the USA on acid-free paper.
Order online: www.finishinglinepress.com
            also available on amazon.com

                Author inquiries and mail orders:
                      Finishing Line Press
                        P. O. Box 1626
                  Georgetown, Kentucky 40324
                            U. S. A.

# Table of Contents

...there are those who believe with all their heart that a piece of meat, to the degree possible dripping blood, is the only reliable nourishment...

From "Sins of the Flesh", *Aphrodite*
by Isabelle Allende

# What To Make of It

My hands knead the meat, press, squeeze,
Until the mass becomes a brick, until the brick resembles
Something the body cannot possibly remember.
The onions erupt, little brick-buried daggers, bread crumbs,
Yellow eyes, completely averting whatever they were to become,
Instead take on the desire of binding.

I want to love the animal that this once was, my own animal-body
Wanting to take it in whole, wanting my mouth around it.
Not the heavy red metals that once carried the body presumably
Through a field. The fields were once glowing
And these hands that were once mine, now, detached.
I do not know whose hands these are.

I hold them up to the light, alien limbs, my own flesh
Gloved with the flesh of another.

**She Wants It, Bad**


When the vegetarian cooks meat, she
Handles it tenderly, remembering

That once it breathed as she breathes—
That blood binds us all.

How to deter this wanting.
How the body remembers the tear

Of flesh, the red puddle on the plate
In which to dip a crust. How even sweet

Butter is born out of birth
Fed to the machine of mouths. And yet,

When she makes the analogues, the false-flesh,
They never satisfy; there is something

About the way meat scents the room; sometimes
She wants nothing more than to revert back.

To remember. Also, to forget.

# A History in the Shape of a Woman in the Shape of Something Else

Some days claim their needles openly, others prick
In the aftermath—the haystack, a roll through the hay,
Hey where are you going we were just getting
To the good part where the girl takes off her clothes.

We're not talking about stripping, though, or burlesque,
Except one can't say such things without thinking them.
But it's something closer to a peeling off of skin,
Albeit more brutal. There is an inherent brutality

In every act, the possibility of an inadvertent slip
Where suddenly the needle sticks. Inject me with that,
Fill me with a pale fluid. Flood me with me longing, with loss.
The suck of the hours of the day the minutes pulling

Us through one into the other, until the stitches fail
And the needle stops, dead-ended by the end of thread.
Some conversations are like conversions, bringing
Me to the brink of understanding the rules that govern,

But others revert me back to that day in grade-school.
Take me back. Avert your eyes. And don't get me
Started on the black widow hidden in the apple,
The web-nest at the stem, the marble of it, glistening.

## Every Poem is Not a Love Poem

For the third night in a row I reheat
The rice, stir until the softened zucchini
Falls apart, red wedges of tomato
Stripped to skin, tan hunks of cremini
Spongy between grains of wild rice.
Tonight I add Polish not-sausage,
Subbing for the bite of meat, the tang
Of flesh, even knowing that
If the real thing were what was
Before me, daring, that I might
Still not have the heart to eat,
No matter how hungry. (How hungry.)
I lay the not-meat out in rows and my knife
Finds a clean way through to the board,
Methodical and neat, each disc falling over
The other until they are uniform in their failings.
How the pan sears the little circles until
The backsides blacken, forgotten in the pan,
While I in another room of the mind move furniture
Just to find that the arrangement matters not at all.

# Enough

How it is to hunger, that striated tension in the gut.
A vertical glass bell within the body, making its bright music.

How my head fills with a high relief, as though I could reach
And stroke the dancing animals that have risen there, marble-
smooth.

How is it that hunger can impel the body primal, moss and grass
Not enough, leaves, not enough, juice and broth, not enough.

How hollow we become before we give in, what skins must be
torn free.
In the alley out back, bones jangle in the dust near a plastic fork.

And if I tell you that I love you, what I might mean is that
The hunger has become too much, my body too weak,

And my mind too filled with windows.
And still, my belly, my neck, my throat, aches.

The bell shatters and the glass brightens.
What is there left to break.

# Self-Portrait in the Kitchen as the Wife without Hands

I am that woman who on all fours licks the baseboards,
Each spot of spilt grease on the floor rubbed up with
An elbow, the stump of a wrist. The pots gleam.
I drain the pasta by slipping pot holders up my arms
And tipping with my chin, the steam a farewell and pinking
My cheeks. At the table I use my teeth to write poems
In beet ink, and build elaborate trapezes that I use
To swing above the stove by my knees. I don't
Know what any of this means except that
When the calls come in to tell me that the ship
Is in the driveway and there are pirates on the lawn
I imagine myself fighting off the hordes with a spoon
Between my toes, unhanding the neighbor's
Stubborn poodle. The cat dreams of me as I write this.
The counter is covered by selkies, by mermen.
The carrots and onions conspire in the cupboard
To remake what I have lost, connective tissue
Emerging from their ends like roots, but I love
What I have become, no recipe could remake me.

# Stock

Ribs of celery, filmy onion skin, whole carrots, in a pot.
The boil of a bay leaf, the bubbles that pop as they emerge.

My ribs ache, my skin sweats, my hair falls in my eyes,
I push it away, and stir. Corn cobs float, kernels, glistening.

Kitchen-heat, a glass of wine, another, more for the stock,
Then my glass, and stir. The ribs of celery soften, and my
    thoughts

Wander. Garlic and salt. A remedy for excess kissing.
Don't kiss me. I stir. I sip. The wooden spoon in my hand.

What else in my hand. The bay leaf is lost beneath the surface.
The corn cobs bob, the ribs, my own heaving.

Don't kiss me. I push the hair back behind my ear. The kitchen is
    too hot.
More in my glass. The stock boils, the broth browns, richer

As much for what it lacks. Scraps dropped into the pot
Bob on the surface. What will become of them, because of me?

Simmering, each breath, my own heaving. I sip, I stir.

## Sweat

The brown skin peels and crackles, flakes.
My knife pares two slits and my thumbs peel back
The crackling brown, a thin film, a white outer layer
Falling free, too, until what is left is the smooth white orb,

Reminding me of all that feeds.
Stinging, a sweetness that bites when I open my mouth,
And my eyes clench, salt rivulets, a held breath too late.
And the blade makes long slow passes,
And the onion falls to pieces.

My hands gather the shards, drop them in the pan, the flame beneath,
A low blue mouth, serpent of flame.
The white chips transforming into shattered, glassy windows.

## To Want Is to Wait

Bodies were made to want,
It seems, nothing a given.

Hands that want to stroke,
Teeth that want to bite into.

Meat is a body that no longer wants.
My teeth want it, and my tongue,

Though my mind is a bit late coming
To the party, the streamers

Are all falling down.
The lecherous drunk uncle on the kitchen floor.

The body in the oven.
The body is an oven.

All wanting incubates, though
Even then the wanting isn't enough.

What does it take to carve
—a sharp, dislocating knife.

## Instant, No Gratification

I tear and tip the envelope
Into the cup, the brown powder
Dissolving, whitish squares
Of tofu floating—little sponges
That sink once they have
Sucked up enough.

There is nothing in this cup
That fills me,
Yet still I drink;
Nothing that my body
Wants more than
What I can't allow myself to have.

# Only the Pots Know the Boiling Points of their Broths

In the kitchen we only eat
With oars. In the kitchen there is no noise
Except the sound of running water
And a shrill screaming as the kitten
Noses the child who then
Cuts himself
With a sharp knife.
In the kitchen there are no knives.
Did I say there are no knives?

In the kitchen there is a kitten
And in the kitten is a small child
And in the small child there is
A fist that is eating something smaller,
More like a jelly doughnut.

In the kitchen I am not
The small child I am the knife.

In the kitchen there is no kitten.
Instead there is a noise that sounds
More like a muffled cough but is
Really me at the stove,
Scraping and scraping the edges.

## Falling In, Falling Out

The soup pot stirs, my hair dips into the broth,
Tendrils warm against my neck like a whisper.

I lean again to listen: the potatoes tell me what their eyes have seen.
My own, threaded by a needle of light, squint against, resist.

*Poor leeks, you have been abandoned; jilted cousin to the onion,*
*No one will kiss you.* I will kiss you. My mouth rounds and takes you in.

Mushrooms bob amid the murk, buoy up the blooms of wilted
    spinach.
The green swish in the bowl as my hands raise it toward my head &

I dive in; the splash as my body's displacement sends spray
To the ceiling. What muscles it takes to swim laps.

What love does to a bowl. Bowl me over, row me around.
*No one will love me more.* This, what the leeks say.

On my back I do the deadman's float. The sky is a ceiling crackled
With grieving, the loneliness of a backyard dog.

Step out, stand alone in the kitchen with me.
The bowl is an ocean only I can drown in.

# Honey

I do not take you in my tea, though my cup
Is a kind of hunger, a kiss that steams, that takes the wanting
And makes a tiny wreath of breath
That you, honey, would melt into.

I do not take you on my toast, though my plate
Holds the pale shapes that do not know
How to sweeten themselves, the way a novice lover holds out,
Forgetting that their own hands were all that they ever needed.

I do not stir you into the tumbler, or yeast you
Into something lurching, something tipsy; I do not spread
You across my oozing, open wound.

The hive is a kind of madness,
The bees droning on.

I do not take you in to spit you out, again, again, until you become.

## What Is It to Want

The neighbor is barbecuing
And I want some,

But I can't ignore that
What I crave is initiated by

The smell of burning flesh. How is it
That a death can be so delicious.

Somewhere there is a photograph
Of you holding a leg to your lips,

Your teeth bared. Teeth that crave flesh.
What sweet meat.

The drive to eat, the drive to bring
Another's body closer to your own.

Bodies hunger—for what.
My own is not so different.

## Wishbone's Wish

```
          Split
          m e
       clea nly
      do        wn
     the        cen
     ter        so I
     do         n't
     ha         ve
    to m        ake a
    deci        sion
```

# Grace

## 1.

What is there to be thankful for: This body, this breast
That takes the softened butter, the sprigs of herbs
Beneath the skin, the quartered oranges my hand has fitted into
The cavity where the heart once beat, alongside hunks of onion.
The heat will transform this body into something golden & holy,
A consecration of the elements, its flesh into your flesh,
So that when I take it into my mouth,
It is you that will be melting on my tongue.

## 2.

At nineteen, my first lover peeled an orange.
My body did not know what it wanted and yet the orange
Was surprisingly welcome, each wet segment warmed
As his fingers slipped them into me, then out, then into his mouth,
Or into my own, this rite my first transmutation.
Yet even with this, I did not know what it felt like
To ascend to the top of my own head;
To have my own mind whited out by my own hands, to owe nothing
   to anyone.

## 3.

The porcelain sink pinked with blood: the body's ablution,
Washed and dried as carefully as I attend to my own.
When I heft the bird into the pan, fingers locked against slick skin,
I think of you, of what your heavy bones might feel like
Pressed between my palms. What heat does to the body.
The oven a scented grove, the heat a drowsy summer to dream through.
Bird body your body my body, an offering; liturgical.
What else do I have to give but this.

## Kitchen Bliss

Each breast in hand I marry to the beaten
Egg. The bowl is a white shell. I want

To see them pink as I lay them in the tray
Of crumbs, then again against the glass pan

That lifts them like a developing photo's
Wet smudge. They sing as they singe

And brown a sweet song that carries
Through the house, buries itself in the sheets.

See the eager oven, my hot hands.
I want to be fed from an open palm.

The meat carries a secret message.
The stroll of muscle through the gut

Carries it deep where it plants a seed;
Doors open everywhere.

## Reciprocity

*Osculum conspiratio; I bring you my breath, my lips.*
I take the bowl from the cupboard, hands cupping the bowl.
I take the egg from cold storage and break the shell,
A pool of clear and a smooth yellow disc;

My fingers tangle the two together, a filmy swirl.
*Basium; my mouth presses against my own hand to remember.*
And then I scoop the flour white with unbecoming and mound the
    bowl.
And then I scoop the sugar that sparkles like glass ground fine.

And then I salt the bowl. And I then lift
The three spotted yellow softened fruits, peel and break.
*Savium; with what intention did your mouth meet mine.*
The lilting of their falling upon the mound,

My hands kneading them thick and smooth,
Bringing them and the flour and the sugar with the egg to the edge.
Between the batter and the bread lies this.
*Between knowing and believing, your kiss.*

## The Body, Like Bread

And when you awaken before the spread of dawn,
Before violet light and creep of noise,
Even before the moon slides into your back pocket,
Lost among yesterday's receipts, there is an hour

Where the mind stirs, and even as
Your shut lids conceal the room's ripe edges,
They see, and so you open them to find
The dark shapes are not as they seem:

The cabinets and shelves hover, the bills
In their folders, old photographs, letters, each book
Ghosting, a collage of seams and seemings.
A quarrel at close of evening has again unearthed

Old debts and doubts. And who was that
You were dreaming; whose hands were those
Milking the flannel of the forgetful minutes?
Your eyes to the ceiling strain to remember,

And your own hands, and in that white dark,
The frame of the room, you allow the rising—
How it would be for someone else's hands,
And how the body opens, sweetly blooming.

## Cake

Two eggs
In the palm
Of one hand.

Do not measure
The sugar—
It's never too sweet.

Swans Down flour,
Softer than
You've ever known.

Stir.
Flour the pan.
Lick the spoon.

Add heat,
Everything
Rises.

# The Present, Tense

I am walking in the field.

Morning a broken yoke in the pan,
Mid-day rye with mayo and tomato.

Sad coyotes at dusk trot, find a catch
To gnash their teeth against.

Night, the natty blue bedspread
As you dream the sky a blackboard,

Each chalky name a star erasing slowly—
*Which do you remember, do you forget?*

The field does change, the field does
Turn, thin shoots filling in, erupting

Into bright heads that fall, hurrying
Prickly seeds that catch on socks,

Rage against ankles. Seasons whitewash
The details, gray the animal bodies.

Make your way across this field, this field.

## After the Fair

The tents packed up, the rides shut down,
Cotton candy spun out
Into the universe of mouths,
Deep fried butter jiggling;
After the ice is dumped into the flowerbeds,
Pop machines drained—
Where do we go to own ourselves now,
Now that the unwon fish and frogs
Have expired in their bowls?
The expectations of the hour have reduced
To sawdust and sugar, the sweetness
Of sun on our shoulders as we perused
Racks of blown glass.
How could we have known that
What we left behind then
Would not be around when we
Came again next year?

Cati Porter is a poet, editor, community arts facilitator, and mother of two boys. She is the author of *My Skies of Small Horses* (Word Tech, 2016), *Seven Floors Up* (Mayapple Press, 2008), and the chapbooks *small fruit songs* (Pudding House, 2008), *The Way Things Move The Dark* (Dancing Girl Press, 2013), *(al)most delicious* (Dancing Girl Press, 2010), and an illustrated chapbook, *what Desire makes of us* (Dancing Girl Press, 2015; e-chapbook originally published by Ahadada Books, 2011).

Her work has been anthologized in *White Ink: Poems on Mothers and Motherhood* (Demeter Press/York University, Canada), *The Bedside Guide to No Tell Motel—Second Floor* (No Tell Books), *Letters to the World* (Red Hen Press), and *Women Write Resistance* (Blue Hyacinth Press) and *Bared* (Les Femmes Folles Press) and in the journals *Contrary Magazine, Hartskill Review, The Quotable Lit, Tin Cannon, No Tell Motel, Wicked Alice, Crab Creek Review* (as finalist in their poetry contest, judged by Aimee Nezhukumatathil), and *So to Speak* (2011 winner of their poetry contest, judged by Arielle Greenberg).

Cati Porter is founder and editor of *Poemeleon: A Journal of Poetry and Inlandia: A Literary Journey*. She is the Executive Director of the Inlandia Institute. Find her on the web at www.catiporter.com.

www.ingramcontent.com/pod-product-compliance
Lightning Source LLC
LaVergne TN
LVHW091237080426
835509LV00009B/1315